D1737819

NATIONAL ANTHEM

BY MARIA NELSON

Gareth Stevens
PUBLISHING

Please visit our website, www.garethstevens.com. For a free color catalog of all our high-quality books, call toll free 1-800-542-2595 or fax 1-877-542-2596.

Library of Congress Cataloging-in-Publication Data

Nelson, Maria.
The national anthem / by Maria Nelson.
p. cm. — (Symbols of America)
Includes index.
ISBN 978-1-4824-1875-0 (pbk.)
ISBN 978-1-4824-1873-6 (6-pack)
ISBN 978-1-4824-1874-3 (library binding)
1. Star-spangled banner (Song) — Juvenile literature. 2. Baltimore, Battle of, Baltimore, Md., 1814 — Juvenile literature. 3. Key, Francis Scott, — 1779-1843 — Juvenile literature.
I. Nelson, Maria. II. Title.
E356.B2 N45 2015
782.42—d23

Published in 2015 by
Gareth Stevens Publishing
111 East 14th Street, Suite 349
New York, NY 10003

Designer: Sarah Liddell
Editor: Kristen Rajczak

Photo credits: Cover, p. 1 (main) Ferenc Szelepcsenyi/Shutterstock.com; cover, p. 1 (music) photo courtesy of Library of Congress; p. 5 Eric Broder Van Dyke/Shutterstock.com; p. 7 John Parrot/Stocktrek Images/Getty Images; p. 9 Stock Montage/Archive Photos/Getty Images; p. 11 Doug Coldwell/Wikimedia Commons; p. 13 Maryland Historical Society/Wikimedia Commons; p. 15 H. Armstrong Roberts/ Stringer/Retrofile/Getty Images; p. 17 UniversalImagesGroup/Getty Images; p. 19 Smithsonian Institution Archives/Wikimedia Commons.

Printed in the United States of America

CPSIA compliance information: Batch #CW15GS: For further information contact Gareth Stevens, New York, New York at 1-800-542-2595.

CONTENTS

Boldface words appear in the glossary.

Symbolic Meaning

Throughout US history, certain objects, words, and pictures have come to have special meaning. The national **anthem** is one of these great **symbols** of our nation. Its words remind us that our country can stand strong even during hard times.

5

America at War Again

The War of 1812 was caused by problems remaining between the new United States and Great Britain after the **American Revolution**. In 1814, the United States attacked a British city in Canada. The British in turn set fire to buildings in Washington, DC.

In September 1814, Francis Scott Key went to the British ships near Fort McHenry outside Baltimore, Maryland. Key's job was to free an American prisoner taken during the attack on Washington. The British agreed to free him—but not right away.

Francis Scott Key

9

The British bombed Fort McHenry from the morning of September 13 to the morning of September 14, 1814. Key listened throughout the night. In the morning, he looked out and saw the American flag still waving above the fort. US forces hadn't **surrendered**!

11

Famous Words

Key wrote about what he'd seen on the back of a letter in his pocket. Later, he wrote a poem called "Defense of Fort McHenry." It was printed and later set to music. It became known as "The Star-Spangled Banner."

O! say can you see by the dawn's early light,
  What so proudly we hailed at the twilight's last gleaming,
Whose broad stripes and bright stars through the perilous fight,
  O'er the ramparts we watch'd, were so gallantly streaming?
And the Rockets' red glare, the Bombs bursting in air,
Gave proof through the night that our Flag was still there;

      O! say does that star-spangled Banner yet wave,
      O'er the Land of the free, and the home of the brave?

On the shore dimly seen through the mists of the deep,
  Where the foe's haughty host in dread silence reposes,
What is that which the breeze, o'er the towering steep,
  As it fitfully blows, half conceals, half discloses?
Now it catches the gleam of the morning's first beam,
In full glory reflected new shines in the stream,

      'Tis the star spangled banner, O! long may it wave
      O'er the land of the free and the home of the brave.

And where is that band who so vauntingly swore
  That the havoc of war and the battle's confusion,
A home and a country, shall leave us no more?
  Their blood has washed out their foul footsteps pollution
No refuge could save the hireling and slave,
From the terror of flight or the gloom of the grave,

      And the star-spangled banner in triumph doth wave,
      O'er the Land of the Free, and the Home of the Brave.

O! thus be it ever when freemen shall stand,
  Between their lov'd home, and the war's desolation,
Blest with vict'ry and peace, may the Heav'n rescued land,
  Praise the Power that hath made and preserv'd us a nation!
Then conquer we must, when our cause it is just,
And this be our motto—"In God is our Trust;"

      And the star-spangled Banner in triumph shall wave,
      O'er the Land of the Free, and the Home of the Brave.

13

The Land of the Free

"The Star-Spangled Banner" was a popular national song throughout the 1800s, especially during the American **Civil War**. The song helped people express their **dedication** to the United States. By the 1890s, American troops were playing it at official events.

15

The Home of the Brave

In 1916, President Woodrow Wilson wrote an order declaring the song the official anthem of the US military. The next year, the nation was again at war. The anthem was sung during the 1918 World Series as a way to show respect for the troops.

17

It's Official!

In 1931, President Herbert Hoover signed a law making "The Star-Spangled Banner" the national anthem of the United States. The flag Key wrote the words about can be seen at the National Museum of American History in Washington, DC.

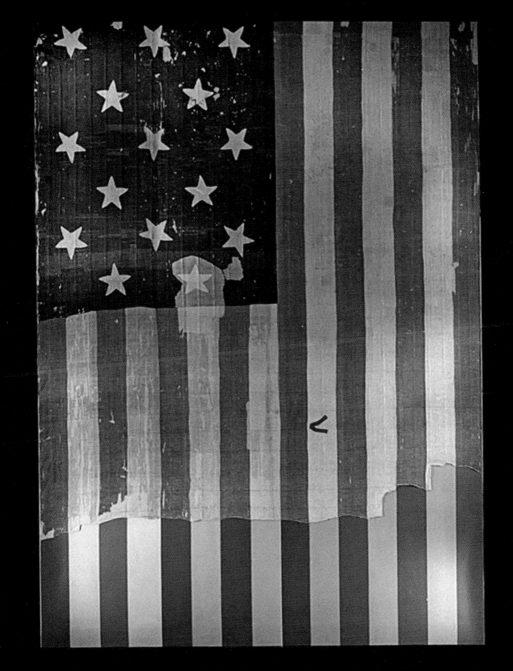

Today, the national anthem is sung before sports games, at school, and at government events. We put our hand over our heart to show respect. We remember what the words symbolize for our nation—freedom and bravery throughout history.

NATIONAL ANTHEM TIMELINE

SEPTEMBER 13, 1814

The British begin bombing Fort McHenry.

1918

"The Star-Spangled Banner" is first sung at the World Series.

SEPTEMBER 20, 1814

A Baltimore newspaper publishes Key's poem.

1916

President Woodrow Wilson signs an order making "The Star-Spangled Banner" the official anthem of the US military.

SEPTEMBER 14, 1814

Francis Scott Key writes the poem "Defense of Fort McHenry."

1931

"The Star-Spangled Banner" becomes the official US national anthem.

GLOSSARY

American Revolution: the war in which the colonies won their freedom from England

anthem: a song declaring loyalty to a group, cause, or country

civil war: a war between two groups within a country

dedication: special faithfulness

surrender: to give up

symbol: a picture, object, or shape that stands for something else

FOR MORE INFORMATION

BOOKS

Ferry, Joseph. *The Star-Spangled Banner: Story of Our National Anthem*. Broomall, PA: Mason Crest, 2014.

Kulling, Monica. *Francis Scott Key's Star-Spangled Banner*. New York, NY: Random House Children's Books, 2012.

WEBSITES

Francis Scott Key
www.nps.gov/fomc/historyculture/francis-scott-key.htm
Learn more about the man who wrote the words to the national anthem.

The US National Anthem
www.music.army.mil/music/nationalanthem/
Listen to the national anthem, and read the words to it.

INDEX